VOLUME 4

The Last of the Unconventional CEO·

DOWN WITH THE CONVENTIONAL –

LET COMMON SENSE TRIUMPH!

MARIO PRETORIUS

First Edition, 2021

ISBN: 978-1-77605-713-9

Produced by Kwarts Publishers
www.kwartspublishers.co.za

Contact the author:
Mario Pretorius
www.mariopretorius.co.za
Mobile: +27 836412000
mp@valcapital.co.za

Do what you can, while you still can.

Contents

Introduction

What hides in the dusty recesses of the mind? Can the past be dredged up to provide clues to the future? At best, the first three volumes of the 'Unconventional' series contained every idea I had gathered on 3 continents. Then I found that by listening carefully that there were not only overlooked but also new snippets waiting to be fleshed into chapters of understanding.

I had visited a new continent in early 2020 and learned in the lockdown era to revisit, rekindle and resuscitate 'unconventional' ideas that might just give you, the CEO, small pause for thought and at best, new insights. There's no Nobel prize ambitions, the bar is set to easily grasped, interesting and common-sense provocations.

The title of 'The last of ...' is apt. My career is, in retirement, taking interesting detours into private equity, banking and farming. There are new lessons and perhaps in time they will mature into valuable nuggets, but for now this is the last chapter. Sincerely hope there are usable or at least amusing dusted-off reminders of what you probably already know.

Go forth and conquer some more!

Mario Pretorius
2021 Bakoven, Cape Town

Mario Pretorius' Biography

So far my luck is holding out. I have spent a lifetime preparing for things that may never happen; the peaceful revolutions and the earth-shattering theories. On the way, I picked up an MBA from the Graduate School of Business (GSB) in Cape Town and attended some postgraduate courses at the GSB, as well as Harvard Business School. My working experience includes multiple-year stints in Oslo, Milwaukee, Toledo and Ann Arbor, Michigan.

My corporate life included the very large (South African Breweries), the large (Malbak Subsidiaries) and the medium. I have listed three companies on the Johannesburg Stock Exchange (JSE Ltd). Because, but mostly in spite of, my best efforts, I have succeeded in business in multiple disciplines as founder and owner, across various industries, from property development to telecommunications. Through the Junior Chamber of Commerce I visited many countries, made lifelong friends and acquired an appetite for learning and understanding. After I fired myself as CEO of TeleMasters into the Chairmanship, I hoped a restless soul would settle. Forays into multiple-country farming, marine diamond mining, (more) property development, data center building and a child-feeding programme means there is some life left in the dog.

My full bio is on LinkedIn and on Who's Who. You can follow me on Twitter here: @unconCEO. My website is www.MarioPretorius.co.za. Please feel free to contact me.

DEDICATION

One grinds and hopefully polish wisdom gained against the solid rock of more capable and better leaders. I dedicate these pages to the many who had indulged me, corrected and scolded me for imperfection and ultimately let me go on to find my own path. All business should be only professional, still I had the personal pleasure of seeing some of the best parts in more talented and more successful men that crossed my tracks, I learned as much from watching and listening as from my own mistakes. It was easier learning than it was to make one's own lessons. Infinitely less painful too – heed the lessons of your masters!

DEAR CEO

We're in for a wild ride, a time where many conventional rules will be tested. Remote offices, electronic meetings, minimum face to face contact with staff and customers – will the changes have permanent consequences?

Business survives in and out of these 'bubbles' – some are even country-wide. Science is being desiccated, truth is shredded and speaking one's mind on anything controversial or perhaps 'offensive' is a social control experiment out of control.

Will you weather these unconventional times? How well will you emerge? The pendulum swings and while we wait for 'normality', these schisms in the business world make for great opportunities to do different and do better while fear stalks the competition. My hope is that you will add more tools for your trade and that these pages will kindle some of your own unconventional ideas and actions.

1.

THE QUICK FIX

Don't fix just 'on the surface' like a lazy mechanic. Find the source of the issue and all the effects. The Quick Fix is tempting and it burnishes the ego when the Top Guy can dispense solutions at the drop of the hat. It's a good start to impress the troops, but like diseases, your allopathic rubbing of the wound may not twist the neck of the underlying monster.

There may be multiple causes in confluence – more often than not. Board papers not sent in time? Probably a single irreconcilable deposit entry that holds up the distribution? Perhaps also an untrained bookkeeper, an invoice system that does not require a precise reference for the payment, a sloppy implementation of the accounting system, no mechanism for feedback on its working, a loose management style regarding time performance or a culture of being second-best. You get the idea. Dig deep.

A zit on a pretty cheek may require more than a cosmetic first-aid if it is to be prevented. See such issues as the iceberg's tip – or in colloquial parlance, the ears of the hippo. Find the sources, cure the patient. Those actions give your entity value for their money, Mr. Fixit.

2.

The curse of the Vagus nerve

This largely unsung nerve literally wanders through the body from brain to the bottom. It controls the involuntary muscles and speech. Strangely, a well-functioning Vagus can be an indication of good leadership actions. On the other hand, it is also a great indicator of libido.

You can see where this is leading. When power and passion collide, Lewinsky's happen all to frequently. Bob Aldworth and Ms Sandra. Mary Cunningham and her boss Bill. The list is long and distinguished, from royals to Kennedy mortals. Vagus workings is a gift, not a curse; it should endow a leader with charisma, not craziness. Perhaps we should look at great seducers and tame them into good leaders? When in the presence of the supposedly great, an absence of sizzle should puncture your admiration and expectations; like the Boris & Biden show.

As for you, a sizzling Vagus is a hot flame that must be used to weld together magnificent structures, not burn cities to crisp. Power without control is a sure accident in the making.

Creativity also seems to be a Vagus boosted attribute. This may explain the unlikely charms of a Jagger and Picasso or the 2nd husband of Marilyn. Beware then when you are briefing the marketing department, it is likely that these hot-shots could out-vagus you and your ideas. Expect that – it's for the good of the organization.

Just don't give in to the curse, keep control no matter how much on fire you may become. Else you may want to find very appreciative company in your life that could help ride your rocker safely.

3.

CRITICAL COMPONENTS IN YOUR BUSINESS, IF IT FAILS THEN DISASTER

Listing the critical components in a luxury car that could leave you stranded at any point in time is a sobering thought. From unlikely to the probable, the possibility of disaster lurks behind the pleasing shape. Ranging from a tyre valve to a tie-rod crack, it is amazing that from the 10,000 components that make up the Porsche Cayenne, there must be 500 or so that splutter between you and the road-assist call. What makes you trust the complication to not fail is the lowered probability of any or a series of failures. It took Porsche about 80 years and a few hundred thousand tries to get it almost right. Sometimes a wayward prop shaft sensor still decides it's time to shut down the engine and spoil your trip.

Your company? List of the critical components in failure that could shut it down for an hour, a week, forever? Imagine a ransomware attack on your billing system. You'd hope the disaster recovery is uninfected. Resignation of your COO. Succession in the pipeline? What about the more mundane stuff that can knock your kilter, how long is your list of risks and what are the probabilities of each? What is the time lag and cost to implement the hopefully in-place solution?

When losing a CEO, getting surprised by the non-payment of the major client or receiving an enforced lockdown order, the adrenalin spike is not good enough to restore order and confidence. Many issues have difficult or expensive Plan B's in the wings; electricity grid destruction or a solar EMP pulse will knock your industry equally as much.

You don't carry a trunk full of spares, but you know where to find effective help. How will your corporate mechanics cope – and what must they look out for on your speedy journey to success?

4.

Eliminate causes from most probable/easiest to more improbable

Staring under the bonnet when stalled raises dozens of possible causes. Your common sense and experience would have pared a 90% chance to only two factors: fuel or electrical malfunction. The potpourri of lesser causes are secondary in the line-up of culprits.

Generally corporate issues that knock urgently on your open door come in two or so main flavours. You would recognise these by now and it is best to eliminate the probably causes from obvious down to exotic. In telecoms a reported fault means someone fiddled with a perfect installation, one of our or a soon-to-be outlaws. Else a break in infrastructure, usually temporary. Then count on an equipment failure – and this is already in the last 10% of probabilities.

In stock farming the same rule applies; animal hurt, animal lost, then all other factors. In mining the same; confusion of contradictory orders, neglectful actions and then the rest.

What are the causes for these majority events? Surely if you can nail the causes you would have a clean slate for your Fixing Teams? Again it comes down to teasing out the one or two most probable trip-up's for the Big Issues.

In telco's; who fiddled – and why? Changing the process of first obtaining a directive from the HQ Service manager to even touch the equipment (cell phone video comms) stopped the issue. Small actions, large results for the 90% of what was destined to hit the fan.

5.

Legal AND Administrative
processes must be overcome

It is a hard lesson learned just how powerful and forbidding administrative procedure can be when these are lobbied against your sure-thing advance. You got the contract, won the tender, made the winning bid, secured the court victory.

Now for the second, oft-overlooked and treacherous part, generally spun off to minions and unsupervised: the paperwork. The bigger the transaction, the more extensive the spreading of responsibility for the risk involved becomes. It becomes 'CoverYourA**' all around and nothing gets the nod until the last bit of ink has dried.

Remember that there are careers involved and people that want to be seen to be busy, diligent and pedantic in order to appear 'important'. 'Impotent' more likely, but that's what they intend to do to you. Critical components? Your paper handlers and you are not privy to the processes being studiously followed on the other side. It is mind boggling how ineffective and wasting most of these procedures are but bureaucracy, created in the public sector, is perfected there where people are actually held accountable for trivial mistakes.

Best to ask upfront what their procedures and key approval people are as well as reasonable timetables plus what penalties if their gears get stuck. It might just shine a light there where sunlight never reaches.

6.

'EVERYTHING IS WITHIN'

"There is nothing outside of yourself that can ever enable you to get better, stronger, richer, quicker, or smarter. Everything is within. Everything exists. Seek nothing outside of yourself." – Miyamoto Musashi.

How deep will you dig when you suspect it is shallow topsoil in your patch of self? The swordsman author of the Book of 5 Rings touches on a fertile subject: your unknown abilities. There is no soil that cannot be enriched more – but it is still your soil that needs to sprout and nourish the coming fruit of your endeavours.

Your soil – to which you can add and subtract, moisten and enrich – and it has what you need to start growing. Education? An added tool. Luck? Like the rain. Opportunity? Sunshine on everyone's chlorophyll. It is the quality of yourself, the minerals in the unmined recesses and the vibrancy of the life force that Musashi implores you to harness, focus and then apply in deadly, reasoned force.

Where and how will you best find it? Trail, hardship, difficulties, unknown paths taken with a increasing mastery of your trade. A thousand practised cuts before you strike once for victory. A hundred plans honed to a handful of brilliant actions. Search and you will find? Yes, but the quest must be diligent, ever-improving and with great learning.

It is said that Master Yagyu once remarked, "I do not know the way to defeat others, but only the way to defeat myself." Throughout your life advance daily, becoming more skilful than yesterday, more skilful than today. This is never-ending.

The same quest beckons for your lieutenants, they must find their best and then surpass it in time. Perhaps they may grow to pass you by – isn't that what you want too?

7.

WHAT CUSTOMERS WANT

"If I asked people what they wanted they would have said faster horses." – Henry Ford quipped.

You've seen that blank stare many times before; the entrepreneurial thing gone wrong. The better mousetrap when no-one cared about having less mice. Reality is that few of the non-horse ideas get accepted in time to change the entrenched choices. Gartner shows that tech takes about a decade to mature for general acceptance. It might be an answer for a problem that doesn't exist – yet.

There is a good chance that you thumped the steering wheel in anger or disgust when your best laid plans did not survive the first contact with the market. A hard enough whack will pop the airbag. Be gentle on yourself. How many passes to set up a goal in football? You may think about yourself as the Sniper-In-Charge; reality may have moved on.

What would a good hit rate look like for successful ideas? In management changes where the execution is changed for improvement you expect a 90% success. At 75% you are a genius implementer. Take a win at 50%. That's the level of resistance, reluctance and revulsion at the coalface.

What do you know about the real work done when checking out emergency orders to a courier company for a new client? Exactly, the realm of management thinking in terms of efficiency and effectiveness is no magic wand. It is often more a whip of needless compliance forcing.

Face the leadership changes: it's Pacman on steroids. It is your idea, it is different and even controversial. You won't fire yourself for getting it wrong but the infantry may not see victory or medals yet. Then there is every potential customer that may not share your enthusiasm of moving your ideas to the top of their to-do list. Yawn. The hit-rate? Probably zero to start with and that is generous. It could have been a revolt or worse.

What does it take to inch up to at least double digits? Big, Swinging One's and time, perseverance, improvement, commitment, focus – all the stuff that good relationships need as you want to be the new choice in an existing embrace. Better be better than just better, better be an unmissable choice.

8.

Addition vs Subtraction

Living a healthy life is one of your primary concerns but not always conquered. A worthwhile health practitioner may give you two lists to improve your health.

The first is a list of things NOT to do, on the other she may prescribe things to add. Depending of the severity of your un-health, the first, subtractive list may well be the more important one. Stop smoking. Quit worrying yourself into stress. Stop the vegetable oil intake. Cut the sugar. This list will have the largest benefits to your health and ironically it will be much easier to do than list 2.

Here you will find the compulsions. Get more exercise. Go for the colonoscopy. Eat the healthy foods. Take a long vacation. Read more. Limit the sedentary TV watching. The list will go on. The point is the same in the business. Subtractive actions are easier. They are instant and meaningful as opposed to the more difficult extra actions needed for the additive. Stop doing the stupid stuff. Easy on the new initiatives.

We all know the pain and often futility of budgets. The negotiation begins before the first spreadsheet is opened. Stop this. Set a reasonable but tough number on the dividend that must be paid. Let them figure out how to get there. Find the most hated processes and humanize them. Stop giving risky credit for sales. Stop quoting for everything. Stop customising for unimportant clients.

Start your subtraction and after the smiles become permanent, start with the additive.

9.

'CAN DO – WILL DO' GAP IS GETTING BIGGER IN BOTH DIRECTIONS

Are we evolving to better beings – or are humans devolving? Given that Cro-Magnon, the first real human had a higher cranial capacity that Homo sapiens sapiens, I will opt for the latter. They don't make them like they used to anymore. The Teddy Roosevelt's vs the Joe Biden's? Andrew Carnegie vs Elon Musk? Interesting thoughts but perhaps environment beats inheritance in the workshop – at least in this can/will do axis.

The downside of 'empowering' workers to take charge of their lives is that a slip in the acceptance of taking orders start showing up. Weigh up the benefits and consequences; in an obedient can-do/will-do quadrant, there may be little incentive to improve the task. It's the can-do/won't-do that generally elicits the hierarchical penalty system into persuasive compliance and has done so for ages.

What's worrying is the can't/won't sector when expectations for a good outcome exists. It's not just the deployment of incompetents in governmental agencies that can drive sane people to irrational acts, it is the hidden problem in the firm that landmines the path to glory. Is testing stated, expected and paid-for competence annually a prerequisite in your business? If not, you are assuming a competent HR and an optimal skill deployment. What can/cannot and should the 2nd bookkeeper do?

Seen a done-from-scratch presentation document from every salesperson? Checked how a storeman does an inventory reconciliation? Seems that the reluctance to 'offend' someone by testing and questioning their competencies in both speed and quality is a new disease. Stamp it out.

Train or replace, improve and promote – every soldier is continuously tested on his skills, from rifle assembly to obstacle course completion. You troops should relish in showing off how good they are. Go test them and cool the champagne in anticipation.

10.

Do problems 'disappear'?

Yes and remarkably often too. Some morph due to your better understanding and changing circumstances. That is like money from home, a win by waiting the way Scipio outlasted Hannibal over 4 long years. Some problems never make to top-3 Urgent list and wither on the vine, never quite letting go but reasonably harmless.

While some issues may vaporise spontaneously, those that recur indicate a metastasizing killer; deal with these as a priority. You wouldn't want to deal with old news in the future -again. It begs the question too: what is a problem and when is it only a nuisance?

The thumb rule is: if this escalates, what will the impact be? Unescalating events are nuisances. Parking area disputes, unreconcilable petty cash and the like. Worth delegating really low down and with an incentive. It should disappear too.

11.

Occasional mistakes – own up

Take some public gambles for small issues. If you win, you may seem to walk on water. If you lose, your public apology with good humour will add to your credibility. Encourage your guys to do the same: announce their challenge and own up afterwards; you will be able to see the fire burning bright in some of them.

The introverts may resent this but hey, they're a team, right? Goose and gander here, we all want to see what you're capable of stretching to, too. Non-players? There is surely a place for them out there in the wide world of non-believers in you style of improvement management.

Few are perfect – perhaps you've met someone like that – and they are not to be trusted. We real humans screw up more often than we score big. There is no shame in learning and getting experience.

The shame is in not passing on the lessons. Owning your successes earns you recognition. Owning up to your failures earns you respect. A little showing of the scars, sharing of the hilarity of undiluted stupidity and the hero's tale of surviving in the nick of time may endear you to fellow travellers.

It is a bit unconventional to self-deprecate but its more real than flashing Hermes' wings on the ankles as a cloud-walker. Polish those stories but keep them truthful and funny. If you, Adonis, could survive such happenstances, there is hope for the faint-hearted who quit one mistake too soon.

12.

On Over-concentration

It is a new word for an old condition. Nowadays the 'silo' concept describes the artificial Chinese walls of non-contact between departments. Here is overconcentration by the individual to the detriment of his peers and other departments that could benefit from his insights, knowledge or at least data.

Sales do not speak to finance unless budget battles rage. Do accountants keep track of the sales pipeline to update the cashflow forecast? Only in corporate dreams. It is laudable that a functionary achieves the limits of his job description but unproductive if there is no sharing for understanding with other departments, managers or interested parties.

The reluctance to be trivialised or misunderstood could hamper such spontaneous interactions, your coaching and support for colouring in the extent of the glue of the firm is the magic wand here.

From time to time, teams of sales, operations, debtors and finance were set up and had to share spaces next to each other. It engenders openness but requires many carrots to pull this fluffy out of the hat. The years of spending time in departments are tough tank traps to overcome. Overconcentration is relative and relieved by a little sharing.

13.

How many changes at once?

Spoiler alert: One BIG one and a line up of supporting changes at best. 'Change' keeps featuring in these pages, more often than any other topic. Leadership means 'change' – where needed. Where might that be?

A multiply injured patient on the operating table begs the question: where to start? Critical functions to save, first, probably heart and lungs before bladder and liver. The first rule is that the patient must be put into a stable condition before any scalpels are drawn. Take your cue from the surgeon: stability first (the management function) and keep the patient in a operation-survivable state.

Thereafter the cuts, stitching and improvements. After each procedure, check for survivability. Tummy tucks and kidney transplants occur in the same general region but will hardly be done under the same operation. The patient needs some convalescing times with pretty ego-boosting nurses to get his waterworks working before lesser cosmetic but still important procedures can commence.

Spread the risk of non-recovery over time. Let the patient get the use and hang of the major invasive's first before niggling the lesser evils. Big cut, healing time, little nips, tucks and voilà – perfection!

14.

Is chaos is a ladder?

Perhaps this metaphor is a little overstated but there is a ring of truth to it. It takes a brave soul to look for opportunity instead of survival when the storm is crashing in the walls.

Perhaps a one-two punch from staying alive to getting on top; chaos may be a ladder but not an immediate one. It is fortuitous if a pandemic-like chaos envelops the entire industry in that it is bedrock building for everyone and the fleet-footed may steal a march on the rest.

An isolated disaster would indicate a swinging rope ladder to jump to – risky and untested. The home truth of when in a hole – stop digging! will at least stop the frantic action and lift the eyes for opportunities. When fleeing, carry as little as possible.

When digging in, retain as much as you can. Your chaos will prompt you into fight or flight, think carefully where the sane line between bravery and stupidity lies. You may not have that opportunity again.

15.

The need for chaos

This is probably not the chapter heading that you expected here – but we're Unconventionals, right? It makes sense as follows: the proverbial weakest single link breaks an entire chain. Which link will it be?

A stress test could determine such a link and it could be a single event. An eight meter swell threatening the breather pipes on the diesel tanks on a ship is more than a test, it is chaos for the dozen crew and a death certificate if seawater enters the tanks. It is this type of chaos that brings out the true nature of hero or coward.

It could be a cascade of weak links that is triggered by the first weak link. If the ship's engine cuts out, a number of action must follow perfectly else all could be lost. There could be multiple weak links hidden downstream.

An emergency event will shows how robust the Standard Operating Systems are and how durable the equipment is – if the ship keeps on floating. Chaos lurks uninvited. The bottom of a scrum is dangerous territory but a game can be won by dominance there. The recovery of your sales team when the opposition pre-empts your launch with an even better product is chaos recovery. Occasional chaos could be seen as a good bowels purge.

Hence the need for chaos that tests the assumptions of safety. We assume the integrity, workability and effectiveness of systems are adequate without testing the breaking point. The danger lies in hoping that the breaking point is more extreme than what we will encounter.

Should you build your career without subjecting it to chaos, you may crumble at the first disruption. Chaos muscles should be built in the preparation when the demons are let loose. Ships crews are safety procedures certified and have safety drills. Your teams? What could go wrong – and how would you tame the chaos then? There is an optimum point in preparation for possible difficulties but assuming readiness on the day could be disastrous. Safety means survival and should be a verb. That's how chaos can be tamed.

16.

TAME CHAOS AND TEACH THOSE AROUND YOU TO DO THE SAME

In a firefight your other brain will remind you of your mortality. Your gut is a good indicator of mental state and short of expulsion, people around you will read it loud and clear. Rule one is that you need to tame the internal chaos to tame the external chaos that is lurking.

Calmness of spirit is an essential virtue. You have a job to do and part of it is to teach those around you to tame their inner demons in the face of annihilation. This is not a calm disregard of one's life on earth, it is a steady belief that you will do what needs to be done to let your spirit soar even if your karma is to lose limbs or more. How else to meet your maker than in the best mood and proud of your conduct?

The office is not exactly the killing fields but your demeanour must convey the same message; we're in this together and you will do great things with me, soldier. Lead from the front, project your powerful calmness and acknowledge those who rise to that level of mastery, Master.

17.

POWER IS THE ABILITY TO MAKE THINGS HAPPEN

The more power the more unusual things can be done.

No wonder we bestow 'great leaders' with more ammunition, it's that we expect more action from them. Disappointment beckons when the talk is not walked, hope gets delayed and the enthusiasm turns to shame. As you claw upwards, exercise the ability to make things happens pronto and to make these permanent.

Julius the Caesar mercilessly annihilated the Gaul tribe by tribe until he isolated Vercingetorix their leader and starved them out. That bit of nasty history of female genocide and infanticide is lesser known. The man who named a month after himself showed Rome that he could do what was needed and so got the chance to undermine the Republic into a Emperor's dictatorship.

Happens all the time and while the gold flows in, happiness co-reigns. A small disaster in Albion later and Brutus starts circling. That power overwhelmed Egypt and its queen, moved an entire system of governance awry. Lots of power gets you the suitcase with the red button and nuclear codes.

The ability to send your Roadster playing a Bowie track into eternal orbit radiates power. It bestows more power to do even more unusual things. Is power the ultimate aphrodisiac? Perhaps it is the ultimate enabler to fashion dreams into reality, or at least until something more powerful comes along

18.

'THE IMPALA EXPECTS THE BEST FROM EACH DAY.'

You may be familiar with the 'r & T' social hypothesis. Some animals breed, eat and are happy (the 'r') while others worry, teach their few offspring everything and prey on the happy, the 'T's.

A lion can only catch one in the herd- maybe. The lion expects the worst of each day. It will take some 8 attempts for him to down the impala and he will compete with hyenas and wild dogs to successfully eat.

The lion is a 'T'. It unhappily tops the food pyramid and its life is that nasty, brutish and short story that makes good game viewing but darn hard going. You chose that instead of savanna's covered with grass and plenty breeding opportunities without childcare issues. Were you sane at the time you chose the narrow path? No carnivore can give up the hunt unless he settled for zoo food. Is that you? Paraded behind bars in the safety and security of a known and comfortable place?

Alas, if you look around, you may feel the icy cold of tears splattering from the thralls who opted for the Show & Tell away from the Hunt & Reign. Surely a safe but soul-deadening choice – it's a hyped up impala, toothless and pathetic though well paid and admired.

Does a lean, dusty and ever-hungry wild lion expect the best of each day? The alternative is starvation. The answer is clear.

19.

THE TRANSITION FROM ENTHUSIASM TO CYNICISM IS GRADUAL BUT INEVITABLE. IS IT GOOD?

Allow a bit of homespun philosophy. By now you've ingested the 'expect the best, but..' bit and it motivates you when clouds darken your view. Not every day is sunny, and if you counted, maybe there are many fewer heaven-view days than tempesty afternoons. How long can you remain Mr Optimistic in the face of a numeric anomaly?

Cynicism isn't just for old age but the furrows of experience surely trample the daisies into the dust. A healthy cynicism at a young age prevents foolish mistakes but impedes learning too. The bit of philosophy is that you should go your own way on your own path in your own time, learning along the way.

Your 60-year old answers will differ from your 21 year-old know-it-all. Your first CEO decision making style will differ from your last, hopefully improved style. Your path may be that older is wiser and less is better; it may be that your enthusiasm and risk-taking have grown with experience.

Your intentions shouldn't waiver; to be as valuable to your chosen community of business, family and brethren as you can be – and improving on this steadily. Cynical? Show this to those who understand it. Enthusiasm? Show this to those who need it. An old wizard like you can conjure up such multiple facets as needed by questioning eyes.

20.

QUIET YOUR MIND TO THINK DEEPLY

Some say the most valuable thing in life is time. Some say peace of mind is best. In your top rank a place for quietness must be found; on your bicycle when only your breathing melds with the tyres' crunch. Or in the bath with nostrils barely sticking out according to one Gordon Murray of McLaren design fame.

Such moments when the enormity of the universe surrounding your life at that moment becomes palpable, little speck of dust in the cosmic wind but important in your way for an infinitesimal moment in eternity.

It's not important what you think in those quiet moments, but that you think beyond the immediate things, of the wonder of being you in the small instance of a life speeding to its end. From this great perspective, the problems on your desk and jerking at your sleeve may not warrant the time for the insignificance of solving.

Some should be left to wither by neglect, others banished and still more dealt with in harsh abruptness – all to give time for you to be freed of insignificance and to think, after deep breaths, of things never thought of before.

21.

The Great Wait

The largest part of your life will be spent in waiting.

You will have multiple, if almost uncountable periods of waiting for something or someone; these will overlap into a matrix that may grow to an untameable hedgerow of frustrated ambition and soul-destroying helplessness. An early indication of growing maturity is the ability to delay gratification; once mastered you are free to pester your soul with things initiated and pending completeness outside your control.

How long is your list of to-do's? Do you have a list of Outstanding's? Welcome to the great wait. Future events are necessary waits, from birthdays to retirement. It's the past that hinders, the missed deadlines dragging on progress and just, well, wasting precious time. Chasing up, reminding and just wondering how cruelty morphed into the delayed response?

Most of us are impatient creatures and yesterday was a good time to get today's orders done, right? But who's waiting for your consent, nods of approval, outstanding advice or more? Be that god-send person who values time, who responds on time if not immediately, who makes it obvious that time wasting of work-in-progress is a sin to be hounded out of existence.

How can a hour's work have a month's turnround time – unless that person is 160 jobs behind schedule? Things that passeth all understanding – cleanse your world of this evil and spread the gospel in heaven's name.

22.

Gradients

In humanity's progress out of the cave it came across the digital choice. More and more of its economic choices became yes or no; 1 or 0. Things were simplified to black or white, late/not late, correct/mistake. This enables progress by standardization and quality of repeatability. The gradients fell off in the wave of catch-up production.

Sometimes the gears in the business seem to run on a forward/reverse mode only. It works/doesn't work, meets/not meet budget and other monochrome decision trees ending in on/off. It's easier this way as standardization brings scale benefits. It is unreal. Imagine day/night without sunrise/sunset. High tide/low tide in a second. Would be crazy/not crazy?

Hence a petition for gradients. You may switch the air conditioner on/off but regulate the temperature in minute degrees. It is easier to see the world in for me/against me as a Bush once said but part of the civilizing effect of progress are the nuances between extremes. Subtlety, nuance, finesse and interpretation is needed to bring to life the intricacies and poignancies of situations needed for a full spectrum understanding.

The military is known for its brusqueness and pointedness. If you are marching your column in a straight line over enemy defences, the outcome could be less certain than if you had considered the lay of the land and the conditions of the road. Person to person needs softer middle ground that machines are not in need of.

23.

BINARIES

It is tempting, easy and often self-serving to demand binary answers to questions. Yes or No are answers but often incomplete ones. Nature inherently conserves energy and the default position will be the path of least resistance. Yet the unconventional must overcome the short and easy path that misses the deep understanding of overcoming difficulties.

'How did we get here?' is perhaps a more clever question than 'Explain what is going on'

'How does that fit into our strategy?' is perhaps wiser that 'WTF were you thinking?'

'How can you fix this?' is most definitely more constructive than 'What did you do?'

Emotionally charged questions are intolerant of longs answers. Often it just requires a shut-up-while-I'm-shouting response. Keep you professional cool. The war must be won and decisions taken. There are rules for punishment but you need to establish the verdict first. Question to understand, not condemn. You may just learn a number of things you weren't aware of.

24.

The Pistol shooting rule

Ten meters isn't that far but aiming with and extended arm at a very small dot really taxes the concentration. Do it 40 times over and you have an air pistol competition. The margins of winning is extremely small, often a single point.

The pistol shooting rule is that the worst shots in practise will be the best shots in competition. Pressure kills, consistency wins. Better the long game of consistency than short bursts of excellence only. Your corporate career is a long, long competition with many, many shots every day.

Your hot streak may have had 36 bulls in a row but 2 wayward shots will deny you the podium. Four rounds of sub-70 will put you in the money in most golfing competitions, one sub 63 and then par won't. Of course you want to knock records off, still consistency triumphs over bursts of excellence in the long run – and that's what you have in mind, right?

25.

HEARING AIDS

Your vocabulary is formed by a handful of important factors; the what you heard at home, what impressed you when you read, the usage by your peers and various mentors along your educational route. It is expected that being specific about words that the meaning is well understood. Like 'hearing aids'.

What you mean by your words and what others think your words mean often differ hilariously but sometimes just enough to sink the trust. Nuance and context creates the subjectivity of interpretation and the meaning intended can miss its mark. Repetition using alternate words is a 'hearing aid'. Speaking plainly generally clarifies .

The words you use may be of a different class – office speak, management speak or even boss-speak. You, as an unorthodox thinker, may be misunderstood even more than others, as your ideas could be threatening, unrelatable or downright confusing without deep explanation. The best 'hearing aid', i.e. tool for understanding is to ask the listener what he now intends to do. In this way you can guide the behaviour and confirm that the seed will bloom where you intended.

26.

CREATIVE STRATEGY

The strategy game is played differently by every player. The goal is known but its meaning for the player and the rewards for success are personal. Players will cleverly change the game and intelligently direct limited time and resources to win. Creativity is a novelty. It can help if it moves the game faster or more surely ahead.

'Cunning plans' are often the Baldrick* nightmare in a sound strategy. Creativity is not a requirement unless the status quo becomes unworkable. It is often more miss than hit and emotionally draining on whomever picks up the pieces after disastrous implementation. Is it overrated? It is unpredictable and a working rule is that after many good ideas a great one will emerge and after many great ones, a usable one will be found.

To turn this one its head, an alternative, the Creative Strategy can be worked on in parallel with the current one. Thus no pressure to deadline and performance, but fun and open minds to rethink what works. This 'Creative Strategy' should be an ongoing project and driven a degree or so lower that whomever drives reality.

A stressless environment should loosen the IQ bounds and the arena is open for new stars to shine. Keep it going even if nothing pivotal emerges, add the new people that join and cross-fertilize with outsiders for more spark. Attend from time to time and listed without judgement: you are only a guest and allowed innocent questions.

---

* Baldrick is the fool to Rowan Atkinson's Lord 'Blackadder' in the TV series of the same name.

27.

GOOD MOVES HAVE QUALITIES OF TRUTH AND BEAUTY

Is beauty its own reward? For *aficionados* of gladiatorial combat of unarmed beasts, nothing beats watching a rugby test match in the company of ex-players and enthusiastic experts. It's like ballet with deadly intent, micro seconds from bone-crushing mayhem at blistering pace, played around an oblong ball.

At the limits of human ability some sublime and unexpected moves can leave the spectator gasping in wonderment. To witness what we cannot do ourselves is a privilege, to appreciate the audacity of someone moving the goalposts is a beauty in itself. Remember the anonymous whale who doubled Bitcoin's price from 4c to 8c by buying 220,000 BTC? One hopes he hung on to that until 16 April's $60k peak. Legend.

Your appreciation of that All Black rugby marvel Sonny Bill Williams' reverse behind-the-back pass and the effortless close of your Jimmy's latest blockbuster sale is what ultra-high performance is about: the heart-bursting accolades of a knowledgeable audience.

Is watching for those moves around your game? A debtors lady hauling in a whopper or a stock count finding the mislaid fortune? Those are their truths, the moments in a life-long game where they excelled at their craft and you gave them the reason to treasure it.

28.

STOP CHASING AFTER BARGAINS

Are there really 'bargains' out there to be had? Perhaps. The better strategy that a noted friend expounds is that things have a proper price and to never overpay, but never underpay either. This stops the 'price hunting' and making decisions on fake values.

Why would the seller set a ridiculous price? Unless there is a compelling argument, the price probably reflects the value accurately. Once something is negotiated for, price is one of a number of factors with terms, timing, guarantees, and the like and should find its natural level.

Bargains may come to you occasionally but chasing after them is a foolish game. Bargains hide surprises. Pay for value with the corresponding guarantee. That is what you expect at the price.

29.

POSITIVISTS

A century and a half ago men in business wore hats outside and suits inside. There was a single dogma before the age of 'marketing' unleashed desires to own unworthy things to impress unworthy people. What was normal then was later archaeologically called the 'positivist' approach and although generally in ruins, a bit of manning-up can resurrect this.

A man adopted the positivist approach of the time that rejected speculative thought in favour of research based on empirical inquiry. Your opinion was kept for weather forecasting. Your speculation was for horse-racing bets. Your ideas showed your understanding and character. Loose lips or sloppy thoughts were unforgivable lapses of judgement and was disdained.

Know, or shut up and do your research. It wasn't a competition to be right, it was contributing more 'right' things to a known and understood topic. Add some of your specialization here, the type that is born from positivism, and shun the self-opinionated banter.

30.

ENERGY

People fail to realise the fact that energy is their most precious resource. Energy dictates the way you utilize your time. A high energy level equals high efficiency. The way you use your time dictates how much money you can claim.

What's so unconventional about this? In dietary terms, energy is either derived from glycogen or from lipids (fats). It is either carbs or keto. You brain does better on keto. To put your energy requirements in perspective, each of the 50 trn cells in your body uses an Adeno-tri-phosphate molecule of energy every 75 seconds. That calcs to 30bn uses per second, and every subsequent Adeno-bi-phosphate needs to be recharged within that 75 seconds.

There's a lot going on to keep you alive, healthy and fired up. You are what you eat and thus become the ball of lightning you expect of yourself. Not only food for thought but food for that vitality that will set you up and apart from the lesser nibblers in waiting. Make it your best habit to be a living advertisement for healthy living; eat natural to get macro and micro elements for full usage from the bounty of nature. Get the edge on the conventional competition here.

Be protective of your energy, use it to live a fulfilled life.

31.

MEN VS BOYS

The stereotypes differ across cultures of when the youngster earns his manly spurs. There is mostly a rite of initiation involved; sometimes a stint in the military or a year of wandering the distant lands. The hairy, unshaven one returns prodigally to state that the umbilical has been cut from the *paterfamilias*.

See yourself in this ritual, what was yours? Was it successful in establishing your own distinct identity? Did you come back the man (or woman) you set out to become? Is there a test to measure the finality of the transition? A small hint: The boy reacts, The man responds.

One is from coiled emotions and its mature form is from measured intent. The first is to protect of express the self; the latter is to mould the situation to his will.

The stoic man, the thin-eyed quiet type looks the type of man and earns the sobriquet by his actions and often inaction. You know yourself thus. Help the youngsters in their transition.

32.

FANCY PLAY SYNDROME

Some of us just cannot help ourselves – when you're good, you may want to show just HOW good you are. In poker it is stupid to play in an overly creative way when a straightforward approach would win you a lot more chips. Perhaps you agreed a price to yourself for showmanship.

Perhaps you wouldn't have to pay it, this time. Still nature demands the least exertion for results, energy is expensive to obtain and costly to waste. Someone across the table may be very much in tune with that and decimate you with simplicity where needed. At the Boardroom table, keep your fancy play in your pocket.

Cut short those who grandstand. Think Godfather; you need 'yes, *Patron*' more often than a speech of self-promotion. A man of few words is difficult to misinterpret. A politician lies for a living.

33.

Ask for Expertise or for Opinion

This thought ties in with a previous missive not to think, but to know. Be clear when you ask; expertise please; else opinions and ideas please. Both have a place but like contraceptive and headache pills, should never be confused for each other.

Expertise requires the known to be revealed, opinion prods the unknown to life – maybe. Be clear that written testimony in reports or presentations must be clearly so distinguished. The ying and yang will become obvious; some conditions are assumed or real. Both may change into the other.

Stability is not a given. Prices may fall. Circumstances will definitely change and so will actions to accommodate and ride its opportunities. Facts are what is believed to be true at that time.

Projections are controlled fantasies. Opinions may change and expertise will, given the many forces that forge the world. As long as you and your General Command is clear on what is real for now and what is not, your and their decisions stand a better chance of vindication.

34.

Start with bad ideas first to get better to good ideas

What is the worst idea you could have in your business?

It may be an interesting contest, make long list. Rank the ideas. Print and frame it: These are things we must NOT do. Add to the list, revise it, classify it, make fun of it but spread the word around; this is the SH1T list, if in any doubt of a decision, please come check this. How many of these are found in your competitive behaviour?

Recruit senior staff from a loser company. Close down offices and work only virtual. Cut the 80% small clients and focus on the great 20%. Remove all titles. Pay everybody the same. Track employees via their cell phones. Fire the worst salesmen every month. Pool all sales incentives for the whole company to share.

This could be fun. The serious part of this exercise is to spell out what may result, intended and unintended. Tick off the Bad Ideas List. It can only go better from here forward, so what are better ideas? Some are 50/50 bets, some maybe-it-will's and a gentle push on the limits of credibility. It would be foolish to dismiss the even-chanced one's but from this you may get the inspired seed, the plum in the pudding, the elusive kernel that may just grow a forest giant.

It's surprising if someone just pops a great idea into the conversation, it's greasing the axles of thought with these exercises that opens the subconscious to free the spirit of progress. Drinks all around afterwards!

35.

CONSENT TO CRY

No one can hurt your feelings without your consent, as Epictetus said. No one can make you angry, disappointed, intimidated, or jealous – unless you want to feel that way, according to BF Skinner.

Substitute any reactive emotion, whatever it is, so no one can afflict you with it without your consent. You can choose to see things differently – this trick is called reframing. Called xenophobic? Don't deny, just reframe; "It would be great if you came to see my project in the refugee camp". Period. Next topic?

Called a *whatever*? Smile and reframe with something positive. 'Boomer!' (smiling): 'Made the best of a war-ravaged world. You?' Only take comments seriously from those you would take advice from. The rest have opinions. Let them revel in their guesses and misunderstandings. You aren't paid to teach them.

36.

Two-thirds of your wealth is the operating businesses

If you're a business owner, this could be relevant. You're at your peak and for planning purposes, you're calculating your wealth – to refresh the expectations. Just to make sure the wolf would be knocking at the next door neighbour while you cash in your chips.

You may find yourself staring at a satisfying number. You've paid dividends, your own salary, dabbled in some investments, paid off an office and a house, standard stuff, and there's the number, in multiple zero's. How much of this is liquid; cash and spendable bits?

Before cashing out, maybe a third of the total. This makes cashing out a tempting option.

Talk about Golden Handcuffs! – the sale value will discount your expertise and that neat figure may be diminished when you plan to extract your share from what you built.

Sadly so.

One tends to think in Empire, but unless you have substantially diluted the shares to the future operators and is looking at only a handful of chips left on the table, the two-thirds will be a legacy and a slightly difficult thing to move, too.

If you're not the owner, perhaps the bulk of your fortune is invested in the hands of others. That's also a fickle call, markets go and down and inflation is always underreported. Will you be comfortable by savings alone? Let's hope so. Many compatriots achieved this by downscaling their lifestyle to match the proceeds and keep a little rainy-day extra.

Well-paid slavery is still only that, even for their kings. You may have unconventionally done better and I salute you for that.

37.

WHEN TO THINK AND WHEN TO SPEAK

Your greatest tool is what you can say that can be understood. It is not what you infrequently think or what ideas pop in your head. Saying it clearly, is.

Articulation is the bridge between ideas and influence. You may find that your ideas crystalize when you verbalize them. Get to the point but shut up if you don't have one to express. Verbiage wastes time, yapping is a curse on everybody and Gladwellian* prose must be strangled at the second sentence.

Think often, deep and different. Try your ideas on a friendly audience first, refine and strengthen them. Use them sparingly like good spice, but they won't exist until you express them.

---

* *Mallcolm Gladwell is a prolific author who is needled for his verbosity*

38.

TO DEFEAT AN ENEMY, DEFEAT HIS STRATEGY

The unsung heroes of WW2 are the US submarines in the Pacific theatre. The Japanese lost enormous supplies; oil, matériel, food, personnel – all moved by the Japanese merchant marine. The US strategy to cut the supply route of oil to Japan had led to the war and the Pearl Harbour response and the US continued to deny the Japanese naval expansion across the Pacific.

The Japanese strategy of expansion meant the enormous transfers via marine traffic. The significant successes of the U boats hampered the Japanese until they drew back and consolidated at the Guadal-canal Islands and mainland Japan. The strategy was defeated, the initiative was lost and the defence of Japan still relied on a diminishing volume of imported oil.

History masks many actions and understanding the strategy of the other party gives clarity to a counter-strategy. The same is true in sport where denial of strategy execution means nothing to fall back on in many cases.

What is your strategy, how can it be circumvented if you were your own enemy? How can you overcome the circumvention, and implement a parallel course of plan B while the fight is on? Some call it 3D chess, it's just a sprinkle of common sense and a will to think through the obvious. Good luck.

39.

STEPPING OUT OF THE SAFETY HARNESS

'Employment is slavery sold as the safe choice but with limited scalability & control. Entrepreneurship is freedom, both exhilarating & terrifying, but with unlimited potential.' – Sven Henrich.

I could not have put it better, so here is a management-like quote that isn't unconventional but good enough to feature.

40.

IF IT'S STUPID BUT WORKS,
IT ISN'T STUPID

What a knockout phrase. Keep your prejudices fluid and your ideas supple, else someone might break instead of shape them for the better.

41.

THE PRICE OF AMBITION

"No tree, it is said, can grow to heaven unless it's roots reach down to hell."

That's a quote from Carl Jung. It is a bit melodramatic but the intention is clear: big dreams may require big sacrifices. These come in many guises. Most important is your time, then your energy, then whatever you will have to give up or forego, then the cost in money.

The giving up is the hardest part – relationships, fun, alternatives and heaven knows what FOMO items may pile up. The list could be endless and hellish unless the fruits of the endeavour turn out to be heavenly.

42.

ON THE THRESHOLD OF DECISIONS

Any effective method of decision-making should have a threshold in time of making that decision. This is the point at which, no matter what, you must commit. A set threshold of decision guards against hesitancy and procrastination from over-analysis or expediently waiting for more information.

In combat profiling this threshold is called the Combat Rule of Three: When you observe three anomalies or indicators beyond the normal, you must make a decision. Do not wait for more information.

Situations can be classified as Green(safe), Yellow(caution) or Red(danger). A normal 'Green' situation remains so until anomalies occur. A guard watches the perimeter. He hears an unfamiliar sound. He then sees a movement from the direction of the sound. He smells smoke. He has reached the threshold. Moving from Green to a Red situations requires three Yellow factors. He must act. So too in the office. There are many situations that require immediate action but the rule of three is helpful in low-level anomalies; coming late, leaving early and not answering the phone? Trigger for an investigation?

'Rules of three' are popular and applied to many situations. State the three most important decisions you have to make today. Pick three priorities from seeing friends, family time, work catch-up, doing your favourite sport.

The priorities may shift from Friday to Saturday to Sunday and back again on Monday, but three should get your attention at any time. You have three seconds to get someone's attention; you have three minutes to make your point after a question. Each of these choices have a time threshold.

'Rules of three' are simple and adaptable. Perhaps your staff will benefit – prioritise and invoke the threshold. Adapt or change when yellow factors appear. When is doubt, use SOAP:

- Stop what you're doing and pay attention;
- Observe what's happening in action, intensity and in what future direction the situation is heading – are the Yellow factors?;
- Alternatives that could solve the situation;
- Pick one and implement – the threshold.

Your pack might just come clean from their dithering's.

43.

QUESTIONS AND LEARNING

When Lawyers use question, it is usually to confirm facts they already know. Such questioning is often closer to 'interrogation' and not much fun to endure in the witness stand. It is not intended for learning but to confirm a certain line of arguments towards a chosen conclusion. Such questioning is uncomfortable and menacing and does not inspire trust in the recipient.

Questioning can be a subtle power play and it cuts both ways. The Board may pursue a certain agenda through questioning instead of being forthright. Lower ranking staff may imply a negative tone in a question too. The messages are clear but the confrontation is disguised. Such 'please-tell-me?'s are cumulative in, even without any added emotional emphasis. These are the tools of questions for destructive intent.

Open-ended questioning should be directed towards filling in the pieces of an existing situation and like interrogation, best be done with a witness. There should be no 'plausible deniability' afterwards, all answers should be factual and not speculative; remember the differentiation between 'know so' and 'think so'.

Asking speculatively will get speculative answers so be certain to phrase it as a thought exercise else the response may be stifled away from a future self-incriminating answer.

The constructive question should lead to learning and learning is part of the cure for incompetence. The feedback loop runs like this: the more you understand after learning, the easier it is to set the questions and evaluate the answers in context. Certain questions could show your ignorance so keep the approach very fact specific. Only you think you aren't be expected to know everything!

The Master of questions and learning is a coveted title to acquire.

44.

SQUINT

If you're making eye contact with someone you don't know, squint. Just a little. It communicates suspicion and/or annoyance. That's usually enough to dissuade someone that has approached you uninvited.

If they get angry and offended, ignore them and leave the area. That's not a normal reaction and it means they are already hostile. This is effective on most strangers, be careful whom you pre-test like this, your traffic ticket might just become a full roadworthy inspection.

Stupid? Not if it works.

45.

The lazy-smart trap

Being a MENSA could be an advantage and working smart, not hard will be a handicap if you're caught in the lazy-smart trap. Imagine you're an ace on the tennis court when it comes to serving. Ace, ace, ace, game; great when you do that but you will be neglecting your volley game or baseline return of serve.

You get the point. Cruising on your IQ means looking for the easy shots, building inertia and avoiding the floaters and spin that spells concentration and possible failure. Observe your squad; they might have less talent than you and human nature beckons for the least effort results.

What are their easy strokes? What do they avoid or at least get iffy about when tasked to do? You want rounded players and you start with yourself; what do you delegate in an instant; what do you least understand and what lingers on your desk?

Time to polish the smarts and get good at those uncomfortable smash, topspin and dropshot irritations that you 'smarted' away. You might just meet an opponent who swats your best serves down the tramline.

46.

Is 'the best' worth the hassle?

Of course! Or is it?

The Borgward motor company built the most durable German cars of its time. They were stylish too and buyers became die-hard owners. Many were driven a lifetime and passed to a son as a working heirloom. *Borgies* were a touch more expensive than the Auto Unions, BMW and closer to M-B in price but were better value than almost all of them.

In shady shenanigans, the company was tripped up and in dissolution most engineers went to what became Audi. Here's a tale of jealousy, of perhaps over-engineering outside of consumer culture and the unintended liquidity crisis tore a magnificent marque to shreds. This has been repeated many times in this industry: Duesenberg, Studebaker, Rolls-Royce, Maserati – being the 'best' came at the ultimate cost.

You're not in that game, so where does you 'good enough' intersect the cliff of 'becoming the best'?

47.

Spending time & money

Maybe you're spending time to save money when you should be spending money to save time. There is a thumb-rule to know when to invest and when to roll up more sleeves. It's not black and white, but you can discern about 18,000 shades of grey; the first question is 'what does the future of this task look like?'

If it looks problematic, increasingly complex, heavy on the thinking side and increasingly difficult to assign, you will be tempted to throw money at it. Don't – you have to break down the task into discrete parts that differ.

Every part must be evaluated if it can be simplified further or automated. There should be some brow-furrowing bits left, which are now fed by the pre-digested automation.

Simplicating a difficulty means stripping the clunky, time-demanding but repetitious parts off the core. Time to dedicate to the real outcome is expensive, precious and in professional short supply. The experts luxuriate in dusting these off and detest the run-up. Make their lives a pleasure for benefit all around.

48.

RADICAL VS GOOD SOLUTIONS

Knock-out boxing punches are spectacular. It boosts the adrenalin in the onlookers, heightens the mood and sways opinion drastically. Yet they are uncommon in the sense that there's a haymaker for maybe every thousand punches thrown in the ring. When it lands, it's final but there are dozens of misses and multiples in every round.

A radical solution it truly is – but opportunistic. Better settle for a good solution and get many of them done instead of scouting for the opportunity of a legendary finish. Ask Gene Tunney. He jabbed Dempsey to exasperation – twice.

Floating like a butterfly has obvious benefits but the bee doesn't attack with a bazooka, it stings. Still better, wasp it multiple times instead of sacrificing your life. Good decisions become a rhythm, and your crew will get used to your small successes.

Unlike the prize fighter, you can often remake a decision into a better one, and carefully await the opening to uppercut to fame. Jab, hook, straight left, overhander – all parts of attack and so are bob, weave, duck, counterpunch, step back, crouch, ropes and feint part of defence; all good solutions for sticky situations. Do not save yourself hoping for a radical to present itself. Keep chipping at the goal as if it would never come true.

49.

DECISIONS AND DETAILS

Naysayers can scupper a boat barely launched. The most effective way used is to find impossibly difficult or calamitous details that project disaster on the plan. Split the two concepts ab initio – the Plan comes first and the Details will follow – that's what people are paid to figure out and implement with gusto.

JFK didn't foresee the Saturn V rocket nor the escape hatches on the LEM. He decided that the Russkies would be petrified of a landing by 1969. Almost everything was impossible at that time – for a time. Let's say you believe the footsteps on Luna are real. You would have to admit that time, money and effort can move, well, moon rocks.

Basta to the eye-popping non-detail. If your crew believe in the plan, you would want to give it a shot; else they may not like their new employers so much. The details hide the devil but that's to be overcome for salvation.

50.

WHAT QUALITIES DETERMINE SUCCESS?

The wages in Finance, Law and Sales are high because the supply of people who have the Intelligence AND Stress Tolerance AND Ruthlessness AND Cunning (social skills) to be capable of doing the work effectively is very low.

Read this again.

These are the four aspects that need to be present for success. There's no nice guy description that is real in the Free Market. What is the balance between the factors?

Intelligence is perpetually needed.

Cunning in assessing the value, intention and truthfulness of every interaction; personal or otherwise and has to be called up at will.

Ruthlessness is a spice, not a nourishment – it is the occasional decisive action of dominance to obtain the lion's share.

Stress tolerance is the unspoken fuel, the ability to endure, persevere, show fortitude and succeed.

51.

PERSPICACITY

Is the ability to understand things quickly and make accurate judgments. That should be you.

52.

Starting poor

Poor is relative but real. The benefit to growing up and being poor is the sharpness and shrewdness that comes with fighting to survive. The cost is having little freedom to do things.

The benefit to having of money is the freedom to buy things. The cost is the threat comfort poses to vigilance, drive and resourcefulness. Poor may be your past and is a fantastic learning experience once you've shaken it off and heeded its lessons.

Look for these traits in those around you. Honour such accomplishments of the champions who overcame dire circumstances. Invariably their will to succeed and remain successful will shape attitude, decision, commitment and loyalty. Don't disappoint them.

53.

High pain threshold

Pain is relative – to how much of it you have experienced before. That 100% is dependent on the absolute limit by which your children came into the world or another debilitating event.

Your own psychological limit must be jacked way beyond what is uncomfortable. Your back is the broadest, your resilience the highest and your example of a thrust-out chin the most inspiring. What scares you? Much less than you imagined. What hurts? A high threshold means you can control the emotion and its display. Whiner? Finger-pointer or someone that steps out of the firing line?

That can't be you. You would have to prepare a bit in order not to flinch or pull back when the heat becomes unbearable. Fear never created a hero. The first one to blink may lose. You're not to be bullied no matter what crunches your family jewels.

54.

EMBRACE, ENFOLD, EXTINGUISH

The Jesuits are an extraordinary force. Formed under Isabella and Ferdinand's reign of Portuguese Inquisition infamy, the Society of Jesus was formed by conversos – supposedly recanted Jews. In their long and mostly secret and low key history, the Jesuits have shaped the world in unprecedented ways.

The current Pope is a Jesuit. Many American Presidents were Jesuit educated. The lesson to learn from the Jesuit way of influence over persuasion is the motto of embrace, enfold and extinguish. They formed indoctrination academies of teaching: what better way to mould bright young minds to certain ideologies?

Your reign should not only be overt. In the battle for hearts and minds of those on the payroll you must roll out the gospel and canvass the disciples, convert the acolytes and play to the adulators. You are playing the Long Game, you want lots of covert support and compliance with conviction.

People need to understand the why and the how of what will bring rewards or rejection. Your particular method of this 'EEE' will be a much shorter version of conversion of the recalcitrant to the true faith of co-operation in making the strategies work.

Be subtle, be gentle but be firm in enfolding and extinguishing the resentful maverick.

55.

Work hard when you're young, else you will have to work hard when you're old

Isn't this a most instructive proverb? You, of course, will work hard even if you're old but that would be because you want to, joyfully, not because you have to. Perhaps the sooner you heed the call to greatness, the higher on the slopes you could pitch your tent.

56.

Position value: CEO more important to Board than CFO or COO in disputes

Is it fair to judge a person's offensive actions more lenient in line with their positional importance? You would be doing that subconsciously anyway and it would be the expectation too.

It is not fair, but life isn't either. Get and keep yourself out of situations where a he said/she said develops into an accusatory finger pointing. Best mete out punishment to all parties and send them off for their own version of resolution. Still you will be expected to judge the almost impossible, however unfair it may be.

If you're convinced that you are being bamboozled, your next decision will have to be to find a replacement for the more senior one that forced your hand. Else it might happen again and that will be destructive to trust all around.

57.

THE GOAL IS NOT TO BE SUCCESSFUL, THE GOAL IS TO BE VALUABLE

Once you're valuable, instead of chasing success, it will attract itself to you. That's who you want on your team, the most valuable professionals you can attract. How would you go about seeing their value and attaching a value to it?

Some professional qualities are inherently valuable, and the more current or futuristic these are, the higher the value. An IT person who lobbies for eg. an 'Edge Cloud Solution for disaster recovery' is futuristic. An accountant who exports to Excel instead of using his accounting system properly, is not.

Personal traits are probably invaluable. Truth tellers, what-if thinkers, those unsatisfied by mediocre answers are supranormal. Loyalty, institutional knowledge sharers, fearless executors – there are many variables but you'll have to know those without whom you will not obtain the grail.

Tell them their value. Nourish them with trust. Be like that yourself.

58.

OFFENCE VS THREAT

This comparison may seem just 'semantics', but there is an important difference in meaning. Some actions may be contra the procedures, rules, briefs or policies. Some actions may be a threat. In an correctly ordered framework, all threats are offences.

Chances are that there are unforeseen circumstances. Here a personal 'common law' applies – your own judgement. Offences are dealt with by HR generally in a framework of corrective discipline. It's the threats that demand your immediate attention.

Walking a salesperson out the door immediately on his resignation averts a threat. Finding that person's solicitation from a competitor calls for your judgement. So is downloading porn vs downloading a copyrighted movie.

Threat implies an intention; forgetting to activate the alarm at close of business and losing a laptop without a protective password? Threats are often that subtle, not flagged as offences but serious enough to endanger the enterprise's continuation.

Such threats are your common law offences and you will have to find a subtle way around the absence of explicit sanction to mete out retribution in the form of appropriate discipline.

59.

The majority rules & makes the rules too

Adaptability is great but it has its limits. You may find yourself with the largest office in the building and keen to stamp your version of the laurel wreath on the podium. You are a minority of one at that point. Unless you have them adapt to you, it's going to be mostly their rules – and they outnumber you substantially.

Who will submit first? It's going to be you. The trick is to find what these majority rules are, how they work, what is expected and when are changes tolerated. Don't like the Friday's afternoon off when everyone comes in an hour early every day? Get used to it, it's a custom and the majority rules.

Your idea of fair and reasonable may stay just that – an idea. Even a tiny ship resists the drag of the rudder. The surest way to fight yourself out of the paper bag will be to ask for explanations on everything you find on you To-be-changed list.

The solid reasons will be self-evident, for others a concoction of compromise and incentives must be cooked up that is tasty and nourishing else the partisans will forment against you. You need to get a similar-thinking majority on your side to be able to make the rules.

Diktat may work but why spend the effort and time of endless enforcement? Why attempt to obtain by force that with can be had with love?

60.

SET DEADLINES

Deadlines are time goals. Some say that deadlines only work for those who will accept them and never for those who judge the reasonability thereof. Nonsense. Kennedy got the US to the moon before the end of that decade and back – from scratch in 9 years.

Given the resources and having the commitment imprinted, setting deadlines ratchet the business towards its goals. Unreasonable? Let's find someone else that wants to shine when the bugle calls. Under-resourced? Let's make do with what we have like Mikhail Kalashnikov did in 1947 with the *Avtomat.** Overextended? Try a beach landing on Okinawa before the Japanese have time to dig in.

Deadlines shake our excuses, burnishes new reputations and smokes out the deadwood. It will separate the can-do's from the wanna-be's. Your crew will get used to the shaking of the tree and the pace of business that you demand.

Start small if this is new to you but work up to the double step towards the battlefield. A good portion of your guys already meets the reporting, budget and payment deadlines so spread the joy wider.

---

* Kalashnikov designed the ubiquitous AK-47 assault rifle.

61.

THE UN-LEADER

Travesty? I've seen, met and befriended many unlikely leaders – coming to think of them most were hardly the type you would pick out as top of their game in a Police line-up. Nor would a casual conversation reveal the depth of expertise and competency. Perhaps then, most of us just grow into sitting at the top of the Top Table. Not only do most not look or act the part but the styles of getting the job done varies from conventional to bizarre.

Being the Unconventional is not far from the mean, just in another angle and possibly further up the 'Competent' axis of business leadership.

You might meet the un-leader – and frequently too. Strange behaviour is often correlated with larger company size from my observations. Seems there is a more traditional I'll-trust-you type in charge of the smaller owner manager outfit. Meeting a corporate-lifer CEO of a behemoth is generally underwhelming – my first reaction is always 'will I employ this guy?'

So far few of these have impressed me – real un-leaders. Perhaps their guardian angels work overtime and their teams are incredibly good for the results; still here is the lesson: if they are esteemed and paid that much they are probably very good at what they do. They got there because they do what they are required to do.

The un-leader is just another animal in the zoo, eats bamboo and shoots while we unconventionals masticate on juiciest Waguy steaks. Leadership has a formula but many interpretations.

Should you musical chairs with the top 10 companies around you will end up with a disaster; each one has found his specific niche for the time, circumstances and supporting people. Each has hundreds of eyes keen to see success help their prospects, notwithstanding the often glaring personal inadequacies that is generally expected of these colossuses.

62.

THE NON-LEADER

Reagan. Perfect embodiment. The actor did what was expected to project a leader image. Said his lines on space wars and defeating communism with conviction. Berlin wall fell. The non-leader grasps his role, may or may not have chosen his henchmen for execution but is the inspiring and believable face of the enterprise.

He is not the unelected bureaucrat that foist his Master's ideas, he is most likely the #2 choice that made fewer enemies and got the top job. The non-leader has a different role and is wrongly despised by those of us that carved our totem poles from green trees. The non-leader is effective when he holds the gofers accountable without taking risks himself.

He can move and fire, appoint and blame the up-and-coming as well as the decision makers. One can make a case that almost all presidents since Truman were in this mould. The one's who saddled up to ride in front of the pack got ambushed by the lifers who call the shots – Nixon, Bush 44 and Trump. Looking at the corporate world the same can be said of most leaders-by-stealth. The one's that built it are allowed to lead, the rest posture on. You may encounter such non-leaders and know that the power resides elsewhere.

63.

BEING SOLOMON

Nothing spins the gears as the untimely demise of a CEO. Happened twice in my group in a matter of 6 weeks. One of the most interesting questions asked (thanks Darryll) when briefing for a replacement was "what did he actually do?". After an analysis of how he executed the vision he had and where things were going, small things started tripping up the works – unanticipated.

The CEO is where all streams converge, either in eddies or tsunamis with unpredictable sequences. The CEO is the arbiter of differing opinions. He snaps decisions, directs thought and Solomonises where immovables meet the irresistibles.

In the vacuum of the traffic director, final decisions become politicised and unmade. Pitching ideas become sermons and the brevity of good leadership stretches the day to infinite corporate procrastination. Leadership gears in the wheels, moves the traffic of doubt towards implementation and makes a safe haven where change can be fermented or vetoed.

Even an interim or caretaker is better than assuming that mature managers can make independent decisions for a extended period. It's not being a Solomon – no-one can stay wise, but being seen as a Solomon where troubles can be taken to. The pyramidical-tyrannical top-down structure is a relic but a necessary one at its very top.

64.

THE ALMOST INCIDENT REGISTER

If you can learn one thing from a military command, it is that incidents that cause damage are reported, noted down, investigated and resolved. Every say, 5 incidents may have caused serious damage to property or person.

Every 20 incidents may result in death. This relationship between frequency and outcome is generally known and studiously managed. Moreover, some unconventional units also keep an almost incident log, where the near-misses are reported and tabulated. The same steady relationship also applies; it may be one real incident for every 7 near misses.

There is as much to learn from and actionable fixes to be considered as from real incidents. It may be prudent to focus on the almost-disasters more than on the real ones as there are opportunities for prevention without cost which should slow down the regrettable SNAFUS which cannot be undone.

65.

INITIATIVE

Reading General Erich von Manstein's memoirs, 'Lost Victories', of the *Blitzkrieg* invasion of France, one factor keeps cropping up at many turning points: initiative. Negotiating the Maginot line, crossing the Seine, straightening the line near Moscow; whether his side or the enemy – victory or success turns on well- grounded and executed unexpected plans.

There is more than just good ideas that drive a war or a business strategy. Still one cannot escape the fact that at the heart of the now-glib concept of 'leadership' is the concept of initiative. If things work, manage them better. If things need to work better, differently or when the bearings of commerce is seizing up, someone needs to grasp a different concept and make it happen.

Leadership is thankfully rare, else we would be in a constant state of turmoil. As a CEO you may be lucky (and happy) to wrestle one new concept into acceptance by reluctant underlings in a year. There may be a number of 'emergency responses' where you step into the limelight of change but life follows nature: the preservation of energy is paramount to existence. It is daunting to develop a corporate acceptance of initiative-generation without the fear of ridicule, punishment of failure or petty jealousies.

Thinking is a mental muscle woefully unexercised. Goading staff to criticize and fault their own and other people's current situation, actions and outcomes are fraught with unintended consequences. To prod them into thinking about what has never or seldom been contemplated or done is terrifying.

You need to find an unconventional way to get these processes of idea stimulation and debate working. A suggestion box is not enough; incentives, professional help and accolades should be part of the mix. Some will take to this more than most lavish resources in their direction: these may be your upcoming leaders-in-development.

66.

Hidden fragilities

In a number of books on the decline of empires (Murrin, Tainter and others), a curious thing trips up a booming civilization. It seems to expand wonderfully until the cost of maintaining the expanded infrastructure/systems/technology/ideology gains start costing more than the benefits thereof.

The hidden fragility is the often the ability to continue unabated with Plan B choices. The Romans ran out of citizen conscripts. Babylonians ran out of water. China is running out of affordable energy. How feasible is sustainable energy to take up carbon burning? It is not. Adding foreigners to your legions, Westward expansion to your scorched lands or solar panels to your industry is at best a ameliorating temporary action. There are many factors to consider when un-fragile-ing your growing business.

It is ironic that the British often refer to a business as a 'Concern' and it is often true. How best should you find the fragilities from the long list produced by your Risk Committee? For starters, these are hidden and need to be explored for.

Start at undocumented knowledge. Map the people contacts of the most important clients. Test the capacity and financial strength of critical component suppliers and line up alternatives. Split the financing among three vendors. Establish political contact with your chosen party and get close enough to understand looming threats. ISO certification is a way to map people's tasks around required process.

Data disaster recovery on multiple platforms could save many tears later. Risk are generally known, understood, quantifiable and can be insured and inured against and be managed. Fragilities are hair cracks that shouldn't exist. Expose and expunge.

67.

Jevons, Khazzoom and Brookes

This counter-efficiency postulate argues that the more efficient something becomes, the higher its future use. Instead of using less fuel after the injection system's introduction, car sales increased. The same happens with lithium battery technology – usage of battery powered devices skyrockets and Afghanistan, a major Lithium producer, becomes an important global chess piece.

In a sense, it means that whatever you get good at, will be used more. A better billing system should lead to better debtors collection. Buy a bicycle and running shoes could follow shortly. Dominate the small traders in the East and those in the South should follow.

The Khazzoom-Brookes investigation followed the 1865 Jevons paradox of coal usage increase; somehow we still cling to the handbrake of efficiencies instead of seeing the gap open up. Get good and dominate; get efficient and proliferate.

68.

URGE CONTROL

Babies start life with no bodily control. Some adults are still deficient when it comes to certain temptations. The pre-frontal cortex keeps developing until the age of 25. On the one hand, you should excuse sheer stupidity by those still in the maturing phase – that's the reason car rental companies don't want non-quarter-centenarians driving their vehicles yet. On the other hand, the brain doesn't mature by itself.

Its plasticity is moulded by use and habits that solidify until permanent. If good urge control is not practised, it never gets neurologically laid down and remains an obstacle for life. The only solution is then to actively tell yourself to NOT take a second helping of dessert and to stop having ideas about the new girl in sales.

Such active urge control works but can be tiring and is bound to skid under alcoholic lubrication. Best to look for a solid upbringing in your apprentices where the last touches to a controlled urge-centre can be nailed down instead of hoping for perpetual self-control. Fortunately the signs of the urge-driven are visible.

You can spot the dependency on sugar and fermented drinks, the shopaholic and the thrill-seeker. Avoid.

69.

Can Good triumph over Evil?

Sadly no. Even the Viking saga of Ragnarok ends in the Frost Giants wiping out Asgard. home of the gods. Evil rules the world. The baseness of human nature is against us all. Heaven is earned, hell is the default. What you are scratching out in this jungle of dangers is a temporary refuge of semi-capitalist co-operation in a partly-free market in a changing techno feudalism economy.

If this is not daunting enough, you will have to cope with an entity that is judge and executioner. One who makes, breaks, enforces the rules but ignores justice for expediency. It is your instrument of State, occupied by some ideologues that prevailed on the populace with lies and exaggeration that a shortcut to their imminent wellbeing was just a vote away.

You will be fighting the fallout from the often ill-devised 'policies' that amateurs foist on an ignorant populace and a weary business sector. Few of these interventions are business friendly or expansion centred; after all business doesn't vote but influences for own benefit by donations.

Whatever your government, it is staffed with temporary insanity in the form of self-serving wannabe dictators. You know by now what effect that has on any good that's left, given the horde of Remora fish attached to that body, sucking up favours and contracts.

70.

Farming of people like individual sheep

If this doesn't sound 'humane', you've never farmed animals. Each one is unique on a daily basis – and its condition may change in hours. The good farmer constantly watches his flock pass by and compares each animal to the 'perfect' image in his mind. He assesses each individually without making excuses for a variation from the standard. This one needs hoof-clipping, that one's head hangs – probably parasites.

Is this relevant to the office? As the final authority, it could be tempting to side-step the signs of human distress. As an unconventional, you need to build a checklist of acceptable deviations for your norm – after you established it. Employees in different companies and even in different departments vary, the egocentricity of Sales won't be found in Purchasing.

What you're looking for is outward behaviour and physical signs that signify the need for your attention. What are the signs of a battered spouse? Depression? Financial stress? Office bullying? Can you spot lies and positional unhappiness? Drug dependency of out of control? Alcohol usage?

Have you made a checklist for behaviour that signifies home unhappiness? Animal husbandry is an involved science made profitable by the skills of early diagnosis of un-optimal animals. You pay your flock massive amounts – why would you trust them to self-diagnose and self-medicate in isolation? You must take an active interest in their well-being, however delicate and difficult it may be.

You'll have to find the balance between prying and helping and to complicate things, each of your animals will have a different tolerance.

71.

POWER TRUMPS WEALTH

Both are relative. Still it is easier to create a network than it is to create wealth. What would you do with the wealth to create influence? Buy the skills of lobbyists? Perhaps it can get you to certain clubs that barriers out the unwealthy like the YPO* and DAVOS. Power is needed to wield influence. Influence adds power.

Wealth can oil the crankshaft but unless you're Bill or Jeff or that level of billionaire, using wealth will get you into an one-upmanship that will backfire. Like being drivers or lovers, no man wants to admit being the 2nd best in the money-making capacity. Use your liquidity like spice. Obtaining power needs a variety of ingredients but it can be kept humming easier and longer than wealth. It is more durable and can get you into positions where wealth may flow if you so desire.

Influence is soft power; you may have soft influence in situations where you can be present but hard power will give you the ability to influence where you are not present.

---

* *Young Presidents Organization, a prestigious club for young achievers.*

72.

INTELLIGENCE

Let's face it. Other than dashing good looks or a body that screams good breeding available, smarts are what turns people on – not just to the opposite sex. Perhaps IQ is logarithmic. Some 160 IQ people seem double as smart as their 140 Mensa counterparts. Then a 180 joins a mundane conversation and doubles the average braininess around the table.

The savant in you is always rearing to strut around, how do you test others (and yourself) for mental superiority? One way is to test for a high tolerance for ambiguity. Or not. (just kidding on the last sentence.)

Smart people can hold conflicting ideas for a while before making a decision. They do not feel compelled to get to the point of an answer before spinning the wheels of possibility and adding more information for clarity. In a detail-poor setup, or in unclear choice questions they may recuse themselves for time to clarify.

This is not a fool proof test but generally the gifted do not feel compelled to guess a stupid answer. Put the bait out around the boardroom and learn how your compatriots chew it through. Some may surprise you with that other mark of the genius , the rapid progression to a brilliant conclusion. The US Army didn't enrol the sub-90 IQ squad – they were deemed to be a danger to themselves and other.

This is your ambiguity now – are the slow thinkers more clever than the ersatz solvers? Have fun testing your Clever.

73.

GET GOING VS KEEP GOING

You might have seen the contrasting styles of super coaches, star ballet teachers and international swimming instructors, to name a few of the high-profilers that we entrust learning to. At the extremes, two contrasting styles feature; it is based on the sound volume from the one with the whistle. It is hard to discern which style delivers the most results – shouters or whisperers. This in itself shows a type of Herzbergian effect, kids do better with almost any type of attention no matter what form it takes.

The distinction of value lies in the long-term effects. Is it the love of winning or the love of the sport that is being inculcated? When wiping the tears from a underperforming child who just had an earful, the parent starts feeling the resentment. It is a difficult hope to treasure that the youngster would one day want to coach as well.

Much rather the authority figure that kindles the love of excellence above that of mere winning, one who shapes and forms character with a love and a desire to go do the same to others, some day. Falling short of winning – and for most this will be the fate – should not leave a rage of loathing or a fear of being shamed. The process of being forged must not leave brittle parts. Gentle persuasion to find inner strength and motivation seems to bring out less Tonya Harding, the leg-breaker skater and more Emma Raducanu, the heart-stealer tennis idol.

Your stars? Ready to take your gentle but persistent push towards excellence as a recipe in their careers? Ready to mould their protégés in a semblance of your type of guidance? It is always revealing how your employees treat their kids – and how the young wisdom-sponges respond. It is a clear indication of their experiences.

It's never too late to reform from the get-going-or-else bullying type to the permanent self-motivation of keep-going, but those scars may lie too deep to overcome.

74.

SYSTEMATICS

Sometimes the mark of thoroughness is left by a disciplined parent. It is often found after a stint in the elite squads of the military or after good coaching. Finding thoroughness is comparable to picking up a diamond on a beach; a joy to behold and a treasure to savour. There are those souls that have this trait without even realising it. That person who is asked to find a hidden widget and responds with thoroughness. The thing is found, the reason for its disappearance is sniffed out and permanently countered, a search for other possible disappearances yielded results and the storerooms are now reorganised and the security fool proof.

You stand in awe of an unasked for response that shows a 'systematic' person at work. If it's to be done, it must be done well is the unsaid motto. People like this take responsibility to unheard of conclusions. It's the mechanic that checks the rest of the car for free and for his peace of mind, not yours. There are accountants that visit clients to verify the veracity of sales forecasts. A report may reach you and a mind has been thoroughly applied. Unexpectedly the Annual Report wins prizes.

The Good Lord made only a few in this crowd and hang on to them for dear life. Take up their example and may that become the hallmark of your reign, produce and demand a level of thoroughness that will bulletproof every department. You should get a deep and lasting thrill from seeing the results.

75.

ON MODERATION

Perhaps you want stability and moderation, a slow but steady ascent and a smooth ride to the top. The trouble with stability is that it tends to punish mistakes instead of rewarding brilliance. Stability is immobility.

There is a warrior inside that yearns for more than the good times. Good times don't last in the competitiveness that makes us all victims. When moderation yields ineffective results then being extreme is called for. Thus you will flush the coward from his hiding place. Once a man has a position that is comfortable, he may fight his brethren to defend it instead of the enemy to enlarge it.

Moderation is the sitting duck. Extremism is the hungry hawk. Too comfortable is a trap and too aggressive is risk. Vikings hang around their homes in the winter, sticking their spoons in the thatch while sitting out the winter freeze. When Spring beckons the long-boats leave moderation behind. The meek and timid will protest with the lazy and unambitious. Banish them to the colonies.

76.

Martial Arts

If you are familiar with the grading system for various fighting sports, the white belt would signify the start of the acolyte's journey of discovery.

From white to blue belt is a mental battle – one of familiarization, learning the foundational aspects and the ethos of the sport.

From blue to brown belt is a physical battle. This is where the skills and moves are perfected.

From brown to black is a spiritual battle. The accession to karateka of Master is the display of the embodiment of the sport beyond mere physical perfection.

Beyond Black belt into the various Dan's is back to mental battle – adding to the knowledge.

Your business career should and may follow the same type of progression, from studies to the mastery of skills in a readiness test for the final belt. By then you should have developed a finger-tip feel, the *fingerspritsengefühl* of sensing opportunity and the best way to accomplish it.

The main tool will be the gang you lead and the weapons they wield. Capital, objects and know-how is available but the recipe to concoct the elements into greatness makes you the alchemist. Finally you may be blessed with the trappings of success.

You need to make time to think and think hard about what drives the markets that you conquered – once. Great companies and greater empires fell at Black belt level; failing to understand the combination of forces that propel and threaten. You cannot hesitate at being the player-master, you must advance to the point of understanding a world in motion that affects your arena.

77.

Asimov's postulate

Your dad might have introduced you to good Science Fiction. Asimov's Trilogy could have enamoured your youthful mind. Looking into the future is partially futile in details but wholly realistic in trends. The one statement in an interview with the doyen of the SF genre stuck with me, classified in my underage exuberance as his Postulate: Change is cumulative.

And it is. One diode ago we had a breakthrough. Today electronics is a base technology. There is a steady and cumulative progression from the first Nokia to the latest iPhone. It is not technology that is cumulative, but change that is. Boeings have been flying slower since the advent of the 707 as efforts towards economy started and its is cumulative, probably ending in the electric plane.

Change once accepted is not undone easily. It ratchets up. It attracts bulwarks to defend it. Voting rights changed. Paper money use is atrophying. The Overton window is closing the limits of acceptable public discourse as driven by the loonie Left. These momentums become unstoppable by accumulation.

If there is a lesson here, it is to stop unwelcome change as early as possible. Perhaps your ideas will find a supportive reception and then the momentum can begin. Spot the nasties and crush them underfoot, else the accumulation can change your future. Isaac warned you.

78.

COHESION

The role of the Commander hinges on the best execution of the strategies to attain the objective. There may be multiple simultaneous objectives to be attained but hopefully these converge into a measurable goal. In execution, cohesion of forces is vital, necessary and under pressure it is the defining period between survival and loss.

Most warriors throughout history were killed in the rout, running away from pursuing forces. If the line breaks or the retreat becomes unorderly, the simple maths of firepower directed at smaller of single combatants will prevail. Those fleeing will be picked off.

History brims with victories against great odds of larger forces. The Spartans were renowned for their cohesion and interlocking shields. The Roman testudo formation was hard to overcome. Hasting would have been different of the Britons didn't rush after the supposed fleeing Normans, abandoning of their shield wall. Standing your ground as a cohesive unit is a great strategy for victory or survival, if not at least a start of a legend of bravery.

Speaking with a single voice, aligned to doing business in the defined way; even dressing alike and using the same vocabulary creates a veneer of cohesion. Dealing with problems, difficult customers and opportunities in an accepted, measured and similar fashion creates cohesion. Executing orders and communicating in an acceptable and effective fashion creates even more consistency.

Good luck to those who give free reign to the commandos to do as they please as long as results are good. It is difficult to manage a room full of total individualists. You need to put some reins on your pack and use just enough pull to let them gallop in some form of unison. Cohesion becomes a self-correcting force when doubt or dissent rears an ugly head.

Sadly some ponies will not want to be saddled this way and there are wide open pastures over the next hill for them. Your champions are a unit with different talents, but a force for the good of your venture.

79.

DRIVE

There will be many sets of eyes watching you direct the ship of industry and many souls feeding off your energy as you stand at the helm. Sometimes they may want to interpret your tea-leaves too as the aforementioned cohesion need intensifies. Take this as a supreme compliment and use it as a measure to divine who is not on board.

What you are looking for in your stalwarts is an tireless drive to do the best in any situation. Whatever cards have been dealt, however unfair and desperate the situation is, you must instil and show the drive to see out the worst times and prevail. No excuses, no blame and no regrets are acceptable; choose like Joshua did his warriors. Your drive must be amplified by your cohorts. If you are not viscerally convinced of alignment to your expectations, you should reconsider, realign and if necessary, remove.

A good tug-of-war team uses the synchronicity to gain maximum traction, eight times perfect 'rhythm' pulls weightier opponents handily. You would be the 'driver' in this sport, calling the tactics, co-ordinating the effort and exhorting their efforts.

Watching a Springbok scrum push forward in a match illustrates the drive well. Same direction, same timing and same effort equals an optimal effort. Your word salads must translate into meaty actions and your enthusiasm and belief must not wane.

80.

THE STATIC TRAP

Sadly, that which stands still will be overtaken. Becoming static in physical and mental activity has consequences. Physical deterioration is rapid; muscular atrophy sets in after 3 weeks and takes at least double the static time to turn around – if possible. Sarcopenia is the permanent loss of muscle tissue after a period of inactivity.

The degradation of neural pathways is equally rapid, connections shrink after 3 weeks. At least the neuroplasticity of the brain indicates a reversal and improvement over previous states. If age is not against you, a triathlon in your mid-60's is possible against some odds. Static is a few letters away from becoming a statistic; for your own sake heed the Spartan creed of a Healthy Mind in a Healthy Body.

Thus too, the degradation of your skills – if not frequently honed to a fine edge. Languishing in the splendour of success? The survival skills may wither. Scrumming in the fray of survival? The perspectives needed for good expansion may rust away. Best keep up a roster of the skills and actions that must be kept supple and strong. Adding to these skills is a plus, updating them is the minimum isometrics required to be un-trapped and ready for a change of gears when needed.

81.

SFA's

Empires are built on various excuses for human desires to impose their will on others. Civilizations and business are constantly flexing muscle in the flux of history. One interesting aspect is how sense is made from a multitude of factors back at HQ. In Military Academy circles, the Single Factor Analysis is a tool to pierce the veil of dense information. An analysis of possible inflexion points is reduced to a single variant that determines the outcome more reliably than others. By definitions, this obscures more interesting and competing factors. It seems West Point drills this approach into its emerging leadership.

In business SFA's are useful as a start, but not necessary as conclusions, the old 'Japanese herringbone' model of continuously looking for an even deeper cause.

The biggest cause of human mortality is heart disease. By following the cause hereof through hypertension, obesity, insulin resistance to the use of high-fructose corn syrup and corn oil, the SFA becomes the 1972 US Farm Bill promoting corn production with massive subsidies. Nixon's administration initiated this to feed the Soviet Union in détente but the consequences of corn overproduction kills people.

The point is that a SFA could end at heart disease, hypertension or even obesity, and there are multiple deeper levels of SFA's to be found. Each SFA has its possible cure opportunities but stifling the root cause can prevent the cascade. It is obvious that the 'management' of a situation could be more profitable while the cause stay untouched. Where does your business play, what enemies would it make and what consequences if it really eliminated problems?

SFA is ubiquitous in military strategy. War is messy with literally millions of moving pieces in often headstrong directions. To define a coherent goal, the enemy's situation is analysed to the single factor that, if interrupted or overcome, may lead to an effective outcome. Dense jungles of information is combed for the possible 'inflexion' point of disruption. It often too simple an analysis of very complex factors but it narrows the options markedly.

Manufacturing and expending matériel is profitable for defence contractors, peace is not. The incentive is not to prevent a conflict by eliminating a hundred enemy decisionmakers. SFA's are not popular in preventing conflict. War is a racket in this regard.

Find the obvious SFA's but dig a little deeper, down to the bedrock. There might be a treasure of insight and golden opportunities to be found.

82.

FORCE MULTIPLIERS

Amplification of force comes as tools. Your personal force multipliers come in two varieties. One is things that you can do better than others and the next best is others that can do things better than you. Your network is a powerful force multiplier. Knowing where to ask, refer or call for back-up can significantly add to your reach and impact – if these powerhouses are accessible. Building your life-long network of powerful and available resources is a pleasant but precarious mission.

You need to be a force multiplier to them to expect reciprocity. What can you add that they might need? What would you like to have on your side that you do not already have? The most important part of a solid network is that every player also has his own, solid network. You may be two heartbeats away from a bit of information or a door being opened.

You do not know their networks and will only get access if you can be absolutely trusted not to misuse it or shame the introducer. Practice putting people together that may have similar interest, this is how you build up network capital – by showing you understand the commonality and that you are willing to trust and risk your reputation. Stay in contact, give and share much more than you ask, build personal trust and become the hub of network information.

You can understand the power of voluntary and member-selected societies, some open and some 'secret'. Labour is often organized formally. Directors may join Institutes but the real power lies across formal lines. City of London Guilds are cross related with Freemasons and a number of other 'by-invite only's. Knights of the Garter, Pilgrim Society and others around the world probably wields inordinate power as a collective with possible great benefit should you be in the right place and time as a valued member. Do not underestimate what you may not be included in – you would not know what you don't know.

Always protect and elevate the person that shares his network. Never usurp and always give positive feedback and thanks if you are permitted such access. People are just people but networks are trusted people with histories of dependability and value. With 20 good people in your network, your force of access may be multiplied to 400 and beyond. This is waiting for you, just ask. But always give of yourself first.

83.

EMBRACE ANXIETY

Pain and inflammation are biomarkers indicating unresolved attacks on the body's health. Anxiety is the mind's response to the unresolved fermentation of your to-do list. Worse, these items may be beyond your direct influence and churn your subconscious (and stomach) when you should be having pleasant dreams.

The Damoclean* burdens of your own making may overlay anxiety of the global kind. Uneasy lies the head that wears a crown, lamented Henry IV, not unlike yours. Turn the tables. Embrace the cortisol pumping situations, as shirking these will not resolve your position.

Anxiety is a question to be answered. It is a siren call and you must follow. Once conquered, self-realization follows. Shocks and threats to your existence is frequent and increases as you scale up the cliffs of greatness. Side-stepping would lead only to postponed greatness or worse, lost opportunities for grappling down in order to step on the podium.

There are events and threats outside your reach and worry wouldn't biblically speaking, add to your height. Prepare against the worst case outcomes and keep thinking through better alternatives.

For closer difficulties you need to step into what Jung called your Shadow. Wisdom will not drive you to overcome; a SWOT analysis may paralyze your actions. Only your inherent dynamism that is latent and dark can propel you towards tackling an uncertain issue. Of course you're brave and unpredictable.

---

* *The sword of Damocles that hangs over the Kings head, to fall at any time.*

If there is only stability around you, you could provoke disorder to create new possibilities, some which may be opportunities for you. Destruction brings creation – a fine line to walk but that would be you, the Unconventional CEO.

Afterword

If you've read this far … It may be time to pen down your own ideas, lessons and wisdom. A life that was worth living bear repetition, even if it's just on paper. Small people may one day ask what Grandpa did, why and most importantly, how? Do not disappoint them, note down your thoughts frequently and relive the adventures and experiences that carved your profile in an uncaring world. Make your moments count but my plea is – share them. History is Your story.

www.ingramcontent.com/pod-product-compliance
Lightning Source LLC
Chambersburg PA
CBHW070940210326
41520CB00021B/6979